NILES PUBLIC LIBRARY

Y0-BZY-014

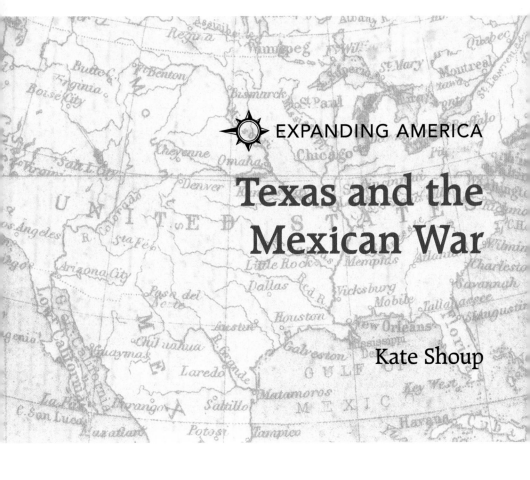

EXPANDING AMERICA

Texas and the Mexican War

Kate Shoup

Cavendish Square

New York

MIDLOTHIAN PUBLIC LIBRARY
14701 S. KENTON AVENUE
MIDLOTHIAN, IL 60445

Published in 2016 by Cavendish Square Publishing, LLC
243 5th Avenue, Suite 136, New York, NY 10016
Copyright © 2016 by Cavendish Square Publishing, LLC

First Edition

No part of this publication may be reproduced, stored in a retrieval system, or transmitted in any form or by any means—electronic, mechanical, photocopying, recording, or otherwise—without the prior permission of the copyright owner. Request for permission should be addressed to Permissions, Cavendish Square Publishing, 243 5th Avenue, Suite 136, New York, NY 10016. Tel (877) 980-4450; fax (877) 980-4454.

Website: cavendishsq.com

This publication represents the opinions and views of the author based on his or her personal experience, knowledge, and research. The information in this book serves as a general guide only. The author and publisher have used their best efforts in preparing this book and disclaim liability rising directly or indirectly from the use and application of this book.

CPSIA Compliance Information: Batch #CW16CSQ

All websites were available and accurate when this book was sent to press.

Library of Congress Cataloging-in-Publication Data

Shoup, Kate, 1972- author.
Texas and the Mexican War / Kate Shoup.
pages cm. — (Expanding America)
Includes bibliographical references and index.
ISBN 978-1-5026-0964-9 (hardcover) — ISBN 978-1-5026-0965-6 (ebook)
1. Mexican War, 1846-1848—Texas—Juvenile literature.
2. Mexican War, 1846-1848—Causes—Juvenile literature. 3. Texas—History—To 1846. I. Title.

E409.5.T45S56 2016
976.4'05—dc23

2015027431

Editorial Director: David McNamara
Editor: Andrew Coddington and Kelly Spence
Copy Editor: Rebecca Rohan
Art Director: Jeffrey Talbot
Designer: Amy Greenan and Stephanie Flecha
Senior Production Manager: Jennifer Ryder-Talbot
Production Editor: Renni Johnson
Photo Research: J8 Media

The photographs in this book are used by permission and through the courtesy of: Stock Montage/Getty Images, cover; Mattalia/Shutterstock.com, cover background and used throughout the book; William H. Brooker (engraving) (b&w photo), American School, (19th century)/ Private Collection/Bridgeman Images, 5; American School, (19th century)/Private Collection/Bridgeman Images, 6; File: Howard Pyle (1853-1911) La Salle on Mississippi.jpg/Harper's Magazine, Feb 1905, No. DCLVII, Vol. CX/Wikimedia Commons, 11; John Pinkerton (1758-1826)/File: 1818 Pinkerton Map of the American Southwest (California,) - Geographicus - Texas-pinkerton-1818.jpg/Wikimedia Commons, 12; ©Travis Witt Liveon001/File: Mission Espada San Antonio.JPG/Wikimedia Commons, 16; Juan O'Gorman (1905-82)/Museo Nacional de Historia, Castillo de Chapultepec, Mexico/Jean-Pierre Courau/Bridgeman Images, 19; North Wind Picture Archives, 20, 75; Unknown artist/File: Stephen F. Austin.jpg/1840/Image courtesy of the Texas State Library and Archives Commission (http://www.tsl.state.tx.us/treasures/images/republic/bexar/austin.jpg)/Wikimedia Commons, 23; Library of Congress Prints and Photographs Division Washington, D.C. 20540 USA, 28, 37; Baker and Bordens, 2 March 1836 (litho), American School, (19th century)/Gilder Lehrman Collection, New York, USA/Bridgeman Images, 35; Photo © Tarker/Bridgeman Images, 38; Gil C/Shutterstock.com, 41; Universal History Archive/UIG via Getty Images, 45; By Ch1902 (Own work) [GFDL (http://www.gnu.org/copyleft/fdl.html) or CC-BY-SA-3.0 (http://creativecommons.org/licenses/by-sa/3.0/)], File: Wpdms Republic of Texas.svg/via Wikimedia Commons, 49; Lithograph by Adolphe Jean-Baptiste Bayot (1810–1866) after a drawing by Carl Nebel (1805–1855) File: Nebel Mexican War 12 Scott in Mexico City.jpg/Immediate image source: http://www.dsloan.com/Auctions/A22/item-kendall-nebel.html Originally published in George Wilkins Kendall & Carl Nebel: The War between the United States and Mexico Illustrated, Embracing Pictorial Drawings of all the Principal Conflicts, New York: D. Appleton; Philadelphia: George Appleton [Paris: Plon Brothers], 1851.Wikimedia Commons, 54, 70; Devin Cook, 28 January 2008/File: Flag of California.svg/Wikimedia Commons, 56; Brady-Handy Collection, Library of Congress Prints and Photographs Division Washington, D.C. 20540 USA, 59; unknown, possibly Maguire of New Orleans/File: Zachary Taylor half plate daguerreotype c1843-45.png/ Heritage Auction Galleries (http://historical.ha.com/common/view_item.php? Sale_No=6047&LotIdNo=50002)/Wikimedia Commons, 66; Alejandro Linares Garcia/File: SignPgGuadHilNHMDF.JPG/Wikimedia Commons, 72; Matthew Brady, 1864/File: Grant crop of Brady photo.png/Wikimedia Commons, 79.

Printed in the United States of America

CONTENTS

Fight for Texas

The Mexican-American War was a turning point in American history. The war, which started in the spring of 1846 and lasted until the fall of 1847, would enable the United States to acquire vast tracts of territory in the West—more than 500,000 square miles (1,295,000 square kilometers), encompassing modern-day California, Nevada, Utah, New Mexico, most of Arizona and Colorado, and parts of Texas, Oklahoma, Kansas, and Wyoming.

What caused the conflict? At its heart was a dispute between Mexico and the United States over the state of Texas. Texas had **seceded** from Mexico in 1836, declaring its independence during the Texas Revolution. Mexico, however, refused to acknowledge the new **republic's sovereignty**. Tensions rose further nine years later, when Texas was **annexed** by the United States, becoming the twenty-eighth state in the Union. From Mexico's point of view, Texas was still its territory—and it was territory worth fighting for. After multiple attacks by Mexican troops on American soldiers along the Texas–Mexico border, the United States declared war.

According to many historians, however, the war was not merely about the defense of Texas. For the United States, there were two other key motives in engaging in war with Mexico. First was its belief in **manifest destiny**, which

The siege of the Alamo, a key event in the Mexican-American War

professed that it was America's right—indeed, its *duty*—to expand its territory and its way of life to the Pacific Ocean (and, ultimately, beyond). Second was the desire of some in the United States to expand the practice of slavery beyond the American South. Texas had entered the Union as a slave state, and there were those who wanted yet more territory to ensure the future of the institution.

Regardless of one's views of the war—whether it was a defensive war, a war of American conquest, or both—one thing is clear: it had a tremendous impact. Had the Mexican-American War not been fought, America itself would likely be very different, both from a territorial standpoint and a cultural point of view. Although the Mexican-American War would in time be overshadowed by its bloodier counterpart, the Civil War (fought from 1861 to 1865), it would have an enormous effect on the United States and the people who live there.

Introduction

La Salle and his party land at Matagorda Bay in modern-day Texas.

CHAPTER ONE

The Europeans Land in Texas

The story of the Mexican-American War begins in 1519. That year, Spanish **conquistadors**, engaged in a futile search for a passage from the Gulf of Mexico to Asia, alighted on what is now called Texas. (The name Texas comes from *thecas*, a word in the Native American Caddoan language that means "friends" or "allies.") These Spaniards—believed to be the first people of European descent to lay eyes on Texas—described the land as "pleasant and fruitful."

The conquistadors stayed just long enough for their leader, Alonso Álvarez de Pineda, to sketch a map of the coast—the earliest recorded document of Texas history. It depicts an area now known as Matagorda Bay. The party then sailed to Jamaica to report its discovery to its patron, Governor Francisco de Garay. The governor ordered Álvarez to return to the region, which the Spanish called **Amichel**, to settle. Unfortunately for Álvarez, the Native people who inhabited the area had other ideas. Álvarez and most of

The Native People of Texas

The conquistadors were hardly the first people to arrive in Texas. The land had long been settled by Native American tribes. These included the Alabama, Apache, Atakapan, Bidai, Caddo, Coahuiltecan, Comanche, Cherokee, Choctaw, Coushatta, Hasinai, Jumano, Karankawa, Kickapoo, Kiowa, Tonkawa, and Wichita tribes. Members of these tribes were descendants of earlier civilizations dating back to at least 9200 BCE. Descendants of these Native people still live in Texas today, although their numbers are greatly diminished.

his men were killed. Discouraged, the Spanish ceased all attempts to settle in Amichel for the duration.

The Arrival of the French

It would be some 160 years before Europeans again attempted to settle in Texas. This time, it was by accident. In 1683, a Frenchman named René-Robert Cavelier, Sieur de La Salle, convinced King Louis IV to establish a French **colony** on the Gulf of Mexico at the mouth of the Mississippi River. Spain had claimed what is now Florida and much of what would become the American Southwest. France needed a base in the Gulf of Mexico to prevent Spain from controlling the entire region.

Texas and the Mexican War

The next year, La Salle set sail from France with four ships: the *Belle*, the *Joly*, the *Aimable*, and the *Saint-Francois*. En route, Spanish pirates seized the *Saint-Francois*. The remaining three ships proceeded to overshoot their mark by some 400 miles (644 kilometers). In early 1865, instead of alighting at the mouth of the Mississippi River, the group landed at Matagorda Bay. One ship, the *Aimable*, sank on arrival—pulling most of the group's supplies down with it. Another, the *Joly*, returned to France with 120 passengers on board. This left the remaining 180 colonists with just one vessel, the *Belle*.

Undeterred, the colonists constructed a settlement 50 miles (80 km) inland on a bluff overlooking a spring. The site was later christened Fort Saint Louis. In retrospect, "fort" might have been too strong a word for the settlement. It featured no defensive wall, and although it did boast eight iron cannons, these offered scant protection, as their cannonballs had been lost at sea. In truth, the so-called "fort" consisted merely of crude huts constructed, in the words of La Salle's lieutenant Henri Joutel, "of stakes driven into the ground and roofed with grass or reeds." One of these served as a chapel. There was also a main house made of timbers salvaged from the *Aimable*.

What began as a group of 180 colonists quickly shrank. Some died from the backbreaking labor required to construct Fort Saint Louis. Many died of diseases, such as smallpox. One died of snakebite. Another was eaten by an alligator. Still another was "lost in the woods." And several were killed by the Native Americans who inhabited the region.

La Salle remained convinced that the Mississippi River was near. Along with several of his men, he set sail in the *Belle* to locate it in October of 1685. The men soon split up into two parties to search. In late December, La Salle's party came upon the bodies of the members of the other

René-Robert Cavelier, Sieur de La Salle

Rene-Robert Cavelier, Sieur de La Salle (sometimes called Robert La Salle) was born to a wealthy merchant family in Rouen, France, on November 21, 1643. In the spring of 1666, twenty-two-year-old La Salle decided to seek his fortune in the New World. He sailed for Canada, which was called New France at the time. He quickly established a village and trading post north of what would become Montreal.

La Salle would not remain in his village for long. Dazzled by stories of the rivers, lakes, and land in North America, he decided to become an explorer. In 1669, La Salle crossed Lake Ontario, Lake Erie, and points beyond, returning to New France in 1670. In 1673, he established Fort Frontenac on Lake Ontario. Its purpose was to aid in the control of the local fur trade, as well as to protect against attacks from nearby English and Dutch settlers.

In 1675, La Salle returned to France, where he secured a title of nobility for himself and his family. He also obtained the rights to Fort Frontenac and permission to establish additional forts along the frontier. With this came a lucrative fur trade concession. On another trip to France, this one in 1678, La Salle obtained permission to explore the western part of New France.

René-Robert Cavelier, Sieur de La Salle, christens the area along the Mississippi River "La Louisiane."

In 1679, La Salle built Fort Conti, on Lake Ontario at the Niagara River. From there, he embarked on a tour of the Great Lakes, sailing from Lake Erie to Lake Huron, then on Lake Michigan to what is now Green Bay, Wisconsin. La Salle then sailed south on Lake Michigan to the St. Joseph River. There, La Salle built another fort, Fort Miami. A third fort, called Fort Crèvecoeur, near modern-day Peoria, Illinois, soon followed.

In 1681, accompanied by a group of Frenchmen and Native Americans, La Salle traveled via canoe down the Illinois River to the Mississippi River. From there, the party paddled the length of the Mississippi to the Gulf of Mexico, arriving in April of 1862. Along the way, La Salle claimed the territory along the river for France. He christened it *La Louisiane*, after French King Louis XIV.

One year later, La Salle secured the charter from King Louis IV to establish a settlement near the mouth of the Mississippi, setting in motion the events that led to his accidental arrival in Texas.

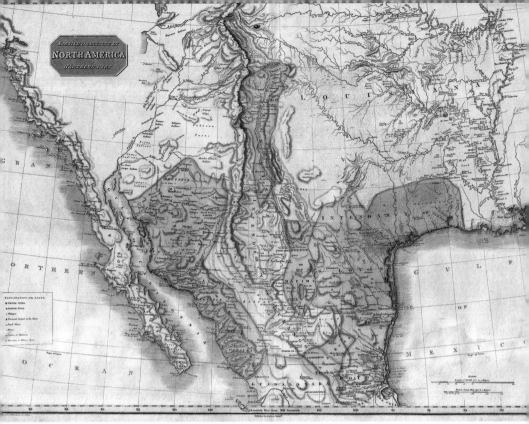

An early map of the American Southwest

party, all killed by Natives. Eventually, La Salle gave up. He and twenty of his men turned west, leaving the *Belle* behind with twenty-seven hands on deck. Then, disaster struck. The *Belle* ran aground in a sudden storm, killing all but six of the men on board. The colonists were stranded.

La Salle saw no option but to embark on a journey by foot to Canada to seek aid. In April of 1686, La Salle set off, but he made it no farther than eastern Texas before returning to Fort Saint Louis. La Salle quickly laid out a new plan: to travel to a French post in present-day Illinois to get help. In January of 1687, La Salle departed with several men, leaving just twenty-three "**missionaries**, women and children," in the words of one colonist, to guard the settlement. This journey was also doomed—this time by La Salle's own men, who **mutinied**. La Salle was slain by a member of his own party in March of 1687. He was forty-three years old.

The settlers who had remained at Fort Saint Louis met a similarly tragic end. In 1688, local Natives slaughtered everyone in the settlement except for five children, who were assimilated into the tribe.

The Spanish Return

The Spanish had been aware of La Salle's colony almost from the start. Viewing it as a threat, King Carlos II's Council of War pushed for its annihilation. The problem was, they were not certain where, exactly, this colony was located. To find it, the Spanish launched ten expeditions—by land and by sea. During the last of these, Spanish explorers encountered a French colonist who had **deserted** Fort Saint Louis to live with local Natives. In April of 1689, this Frenchman led the Spanish to the settlement, which had been ransacked during the massacre.

One result of these ten expeditions was a greater understanding of the geography of Texas—and an increased desire on the part of the Spanish to settle the area. And so, in March of 1690, the Spanish built their first **mission** in Texas, the Mission San Francisco de los Tejas, near present-day San Antonio.

Like all missions, this one was built and settled not just to gain a foothold in the area, but also to convert the Native people to Christianity. To their great consternation, the Spanish had little success in the latter. Not only did the Natives resist conversion, they also stole the mission's cattle and horses and were generally hostile. Soon, Spain abandoned the mission. Once again, the discouraged Spanish ceased all efforts to settle the region.

The Talon Children

Five children were spared at the massacre of Fort Saint Louis: Jean-Baptiste Talon; his two younger brothers, Lucien and Robert; his older sister, Marie-Madeleine; and an orphan boy named Eustache Bréman. (An older brother, Pierre, had been with La Salle at the time of the explorer's death.) After witnessing their mother's murder, the Talon children, along with Bréman, were rescued by "savage women," who were "touched by the compassion of [the children's] youth," according to young Jean-Baptiste. The same women then raised all five children as their own.

In 1689, Spanish explorers located three of the Talon children—Marie-Madeleine, Lucien, and Robert—and removed them from the tribe. That year, they also found a fourth Talon, Pierre, who was living among another Native group. All the children had tribal tattoos on their faces and bodies. So complete was their assimilation, the two younger boys, Lucien and Robert, had forgotten their mother tongue completely. Jean-Baptiste, along with Eustache Bréman, was found two years later.

The fate of young Bréman is unknown. The Talon children were taken to Mexico City, where they served in the household of the **viceroy**. In 1696, Pierre, Jean-Baptiste, and Lucien joined the Spanish navy. Marie-Madeleine and Robert sailed to Spain with the viceroy. By 1699,

Marie-Madeleine had returned to France, where she married. What happened to her after that remains a mystery, although it is believed she may have gone to New France.

Pierre, Jean-Baptiste, and Lucien were taken into French hands when their vessel was captured in 1697. Lucien was made a servant. There is no further record of him after that. Pierre and Jean-Baptiste joined the French Navy. They quickly attracted the interest of French officials, who sought information about La Salle's colony and the Native people who lived in the area. The two men joined an expedition to La Louisiane but soon returned to France in a futile effort to locate their long-lost sister, Marie-Madeleine.

In 1704, Pierre and Jean-Baptiste were imprisoned in Portugal, although there remains no indication as to why. The fate of Jean-Baptiste is unknown. Pierre, along with his brother Robert, resurfaced ten years later in the New World. Thanks to their knowledge of the Natives' customs and language, they had been commissioned to retrace a road that linked French territory in La Louisiane to New Spain. Pierre soon disappeared from the public record, but Robert went on to marry and settle in what is now Alabama.

The Mission San Francisco de los Tejas, near present-day San Antonio

The Spanish Return ... Again

This time, Spain's abandonment of Texas lasted just over twenty years. In 1711, Spain again sought to occupy Texas. This was in reaction to France's growing influence in La Louisiane. The Spanish sought to create a buffer between French holdings and New Spain—the area that now comprises Central America, Mexico, California, Arizona, and New Mexico. (Spain also held territory in the Philippines, the Caribbean, the Gulf Coast, and Florida.) In 1716, Spain established four new missions and a **presidio**—a military settlement, like a fort—in East Texas. Not to be outdone, the French built their own fort in Natchitoches, in what is now western Louisiana. In response, Spain erected two more missions and a presidio just west of the French.

These missions and presidios were far from the rest of New Spain—400 miles (644 km) east of the nearest settlement, San Juan Bautista, on the Rio Grande. A way

Texas and the Mexican War

station was needed to ensure these eastern settlements could be properly supplied. In 1718, settlers founded San Antonio. It was Spain's first civilian settlement in the region.

Making Peace with France

Spain continued to expand its holdings in Texas, building missions and presidios across the region. Sometimes, Spain erected new missions in an attempt to convert Native people. More often, its expansion efforts were in response to actions by the French.

In 1762, that changed. As part of the **Treaty** of Fontainebleau, France ceded the portion of La Louisiane that lay west of the Mississippi River, as well as the city of New Orleans, to Spain. This was to reward Spain for its assistance during the Seven Years' War against Great Britain. (Spain also assisted France in that war's North American theater, known as the French and Indian War. As a result of that conflict, France also lost its holdings in Canada.) France had relinquished its claim to Texas once and for all.

No longer facing a threat from France, Spain soon abandoned its eastern missions and forts, consolidating its Texan population in San Antonio. In 1772, San Antonio was named the capital of Texas.

New Spain Faces a New Enemy

France was no longer a factor in New Spain, but Spain would soon face a new enemy: the United States. This new country along North America's Eastern Seaboard, formerly a British colony, would quickly come to represent the greatest threat to New Spain.

At first, it seemed like Spain and the United States might get along. Indeed, the United States even returned Florida to Spain in 1783. (Spain had lost Florida during the Seven

Years' War.) As a result, Spanish territory stretched from the tip of Florida, around the Gulf of Mexico, and west to the Pacific Ocean. And, west of the Mississippi, Spanish lands extended northward all the way to Canada.

Soon, however, New Spain was in danger of being overrun by American **pioneers** who sought their fortunes to the west. Although Spain allowed American immigrants to settle in Florida and La Louisiane, it discouraged them from doing so in Texas. Spain even built a fort in Nacogdoches, in East Texas, to keep American settlers out.

In 1799, Spain gave its territory in La Louisiane back to France in exchange for territory in what is now central Italy. In 1803, France sold that territory to the United States. The precise boundaries of the territory, however, were unclear. Spain believed the boundary to be at Natchitoches, in modern-day Louisiana. The Americans, however, believed La Louisiane stretched much farther west to include all of what is present-day Texas. This border dispute would remain unresolved for two decades.

The Mexican War for Independence

In May of 1808, French leader Napoleon Bonaparte forced King Carlos IV of Spain to **abdicate** the Spanish throne. Chaos in Spain meant there was little oversight of its colonies in the New World. In 1810, revolutionaries in Mexico—which was also part of New Spain—rose up. Led by a Catholic priest named Miguel Hidalgo, these rebels sought independence from Spain. Although Hidalgo, who would later be known as the "Father of Mexico," was executed by Spanish forces in 1811, his efforts successfully launched the Mexican War for Independence.

Technically, the United States was a neutral party in the war. Nonetheless, it supplied Mexican rebels with

Miguel Hidalgo, a Roman Catholic priest, spearheaded the Mexican War for Independence. He would later become known as the "Father of Mexico."

weaponry and allowed them to trade in American ports. Some American citizens even participated in the war, most on the side of Mexico. In 1812, a group of Americans led by a Mexican revolutionary captured Nacogdoches. In 1813, the same group captured San Antonio, **assassinated** the governor, proclaimed Texas an independent state, and even drafted a constitution. However, Spanish forces recaptured Texas later that same year.

Mexican Texas

In 1819, Spain and the United States signed the Transcontinental Treaty. With this treaty, Spain ceded Florida to the United States. In exchange, the United States abandoned its claim on Texas. At last, the border dispute was resolved, with the official boundary between Spanish and US territory set at the Sabine River—the boundary between present-day Texas and Louisiana.

In the end, Spain's efforts to hold Texas were wasted. In 1821, Mexico defeated Spain, gaining its independence—and Spain's territory in Texas. Texas became part of the Mexican Empire "without a shot being fired." This would set the stage for the Mexican-American War a generation later.

The Alamo. This site would become a symbol for all of Texas.

CHAPTER TWO

Texas: From Mexican State to Independent Republic

The Mexican War for Independence, launched in 1810 by Miguel Hidalgo, would last until 1821, when Mexico gained its sovereignty. When that happened, Texas was no longer the property of Spain. Instead, it became part of the Mexican Empire. At first, Texas was one of nineteen states and four territories in Mexico. Later, Texas was joined with another state, called Coahuila, to form Coahuila y Tejas.

Under Mexican rule, life in Texas continued much as it had under Spain. There was one significant difference, however: Mexico welcomed new American settlers into the region. This was in part a response to a growing threat from the bands of Natives who frequently raided settlements in Texas. Mexican authorities hoped that bringing more settlers in would help to protect against these raids.

Among the first of these American settlers was Stephen F. Austin, who, in 1821, became an **empresario**. In other words, the Mexican government granted Austin the right to launch a colony in Texas. In exchange, Austin would recruit new American settlers and oversee the colony. Under the arrangement, Austin would receive 67,000 acres (27,114 hectares) for each two hundred families he brought to Texas.

To attract settlers, Austin offered for purchase 1,280 acres (518 ha) for each family of four. Farmers and ranchers were eligible to purchase even larger plots. The price was right—at just 12.5 cents per acre, it was one-tenth the cost of comparable land in the United States. Settlers were required to forfeit their US citizenship to become Mexican nationals, however. And, according to Mexican law, settlers were expected to be (or to become) Catholics, although not all settlers met this condition. To ensure the success of his colony, Austin selected only those applicants whom he viewed as appropriately industrious. Interestingly, all but four of the men Austin recruited to settle in Texas could read and write.

Life in Austin's Colony

For his settlement, called Austin's Colony, Austin selected an area that encompassed both the Brazos and the Colorado Rivers, extending south to include Matagorda Bay. He then established the capital of the new colony, San Felipe de Austin.

In December of 1821, the first of Austin's new settlers arrived in Austin's Colony. Some came on foot. Others arrived in wagons. Still others traveled on horseback or journeyed by ship. By 1825, 300 families had arrived in this new frontier—referred to by historians as the "Old 300." By 1830, that number had increased fivefold to 1,500 settlers.

Stephen F. Austin, one of the first American settlers in Texas

The vast majority of these colonists—many of whom owned slaves—raised livestock and planted crops. As it happened, the land in Austin's Colony was quite fertile. One early settler, Noah Smithwick, noted that, "The soil and climate are best adapted to the growth of cotton, sugar, corn, potatoes, etc., which grow very luxuriantly." Smithwick continued, "Fruit peculiar to this climate or latitude can be raised without any difficulty—the peach, pear, plum, fig, grape, pomegranate, quince, apricot, orange, lemon, banana, etc. are at present growing in the colony and I am informed do remarkably well." Smithwick added, "For melons, pumpkins, squashes, cucumbers, and all vines it surpasses any country I ever saw—you have but to plant them and you have almost a certainty of a plentiful harvest."

A Prelude to War

For the better part of a decade, the American settlers who immigrated to Austin's Colony and were referred to as **Anglos**—in contrast to settlers of Spanish or Mexican origin, who were called **Tejanos**—were satisfied with their lot. In 1829, however, that changed. That year, Mexican authorities, wary of shifting demographics in Texas, sought to slow immigration from the United States. They also imposed new taxes on settlers.

Simply put, Mexico felt the Anglo colonists were ungovernable. As observed by one Mexican official, "No faith can be placed in the Anglo-American colonists because they are continually demonstrating that they absolutely refuse to be subordinate, unless they find it convenient to what they want anyway." He continued, "They do nothing more than practice their own laws which they have practiced since they were born, forgetting the ones they have sworn to obey, these being the laws of our Supreme Government."

In 1832, frustrated by these and other maneuvers by the Mexican government, Anglo settlers, of whom there were now more than ten thousand, expelled all Mexican troops from the region. They also convened the Convention of 1832 to petition for changes in how Texas was governed. Stephen Austin was elected president of the convention.

The convention called for four specific changes. First, it urged Mexico to repeal its restrictions on immigration. Second, it demanded that Mexico roll back the taxes it had imposed for a period of three years. Third, it sought permission to form an armed **militia**. Fourth, it pressed for Texas to become an independent state. Before the document outlining these points could be delivered to the Mexican government, however, the convention was ruled illegal by Mexican authorities, and its demands were ignored.

Not to be deterred, settlers convened a second convention, the Convention of 1833. Its demands largely mirrored those of the previous convention, but this convention took things a step further, drafting a state constitution. And this time, Austin hand-delivered the resulting document to officials in Mexico City. Still, the Mexican government did not address the settlers' concerns. Austin—who had remained in Mexico City after making his delivery—quickly grew frustrated. In October of 1833, he encouraged colonists to secede from Mexico and form their own state government. For this, Austin was imprisoned in early 1834 and would remain so until July of the following year.

Soon, relations between Texas and Mexico soured even further. A new Mexican president, Antonio López de Santa Anna, had been elected in 1833. (Although the independent Mexico was originally a **monarchy**, it had quickly become a republic.) In 1835, Santa Anna, who often referred to himself as the "Napoleon of the West," overturned the nation's constitution, dismissed the state legislatures, and called for the dissolution of all local militias.

Community leaders across Texas clamored for a meeting to determine next steps. Should settlers accept Santa Anna's actions? Should they pressure the Mexican government to reestablish the constitution, legislatures, and militias? Or should they pursue a third option: independence? Support for the proposed gathering, called the Consultation, quickly grew. The meeting, to be attended by **delegates** from throughout Texas, was set for October 15.

Before the Consultation could convene, hostilities increased. In early October, Mexican troops entered Gonzales, Texas, ostensibly to retrieve a cannon that had been loaned to the town. Settlers, distrustful of the Mexican army's motives, attacked the troops, driving them back. During the clash, settlers taunted the Mexican troops by rolling out the cannon in question under a flag that read, "Come and Take It." This skirmish marked the start of the Texas Revolution.

Momentum gathered quickly. Men from far and wide—not just from Texas, but from the United States, too—flocked to Gonzales. By the end of November, 1,300 men had joined the cause. They quickly formed a fighting force called the Texian Army, with Stephen Austin as its commander. Emboldened, the Texian Army soon marched on the Mexican fort at Béxar, near San Antonio. They expected to overrun the fort quickly. In reality, however, the so-called **siege** of Béxar would last for nearly two months.

The Consultation

Events in Gonzales and Béxar resulted in the postponement of the Consultation. Finally, on November 3, it convened—although missing several delegates, who were tied up in Béxar. Branch Tanner Archer, a doctor who had served two terms in the Virginia legislature before moving to Texas, was elected to preside over the gathering. He exhorted those delegates in attendance to "to divest yourselves of all party feelings, to discard every selfish motive, and look alone to the true interest of your country."

The purpose of the Consultation was to define the goals of the burgeoning revolution. Was it to achieve independence, as espoused by members of the War Party? Or was it to remain part of Mexico, but under the old constitution, as the Peace Party—led by Stephen Austin—preferred? In the end, the two parties compromised. The Consultation passed a resolution stating that the people of Texas had "taken up arms in defense of their rights and liberties which were threatened by the encroachments of military despots and in defense of the Republican principles of the federal constitution of Mexico of 1824." It went on to note, however, that Texas "will continue faithful to the Mexican government, so long as that nation is governed by the constitution." But of course, Mexico was *not* governed by the constitution, because Santa Anna had overturned it. So although the Consultation expressed its intention to be faithful to the Mexican government, it also gave itself the leeway it needed to fight for independence.

Next, the Consultation assembled a committee to establish a **provisional government**. This government would consist of a governor, a lieutenant governor, and a General Council, who would share powers. The General Council would be made up of one representative from each municipality in Texas. For their part, the governor and lieutenant governor were elected by the delegates of the Consultation. Henry Smith, a member of the War Party, won the governorship. James W. Robinson became lieutenant governor.

Finally, during the Consultation, the General Council established a regular army. This was separate from the Texian Army, which had laid siege to Béxar. That army was composed of volunteers who were free to elect their own leaders. The General Council wanted an army over which it could exercise more control. A delegate named Sam Houston was appointed to serve as commander in chief of this new fighting force.

The Siege of Béxar

In the first skirmish of the Texas Revolution, the Texian Army successfully ousted Mexican troops from Gonzales. In a separate incident, settlers stormed a Mexican **garrison** near Goliad, Texas, in October of 1835. Some three weeks later, those same settlers captured a second garrison near San Patricio. The Gulf Coast was now under the control of the Texian Army.

These triumphs were overshadowed, however, by the Texian Army's continuing inability to take Béxar. The siege there lingered on. Soon, the weather turned cold. Food began to run out. The men, who were mostly idle, grew bored. Many of them deserted.

Finally, on December 4, Texian troops rallied to invade the town. Overwhelmed by the attack, Mexican troops, led by General Martín Perfecto de Cos, withdrew. On December 8, they retreated to the mission just outside Béxar, called

After serving as commander in chief of the Texas army, Sam Houston became the first president of Texas.

the Alamo. The next day, Cos—who was, incidentally, the brother-in-law of Santa Anna—was forced to surrender. He and his men, the last remaining Mexican soldiers in Texas, left for Mexico.

Santa Anna Vows Revenge

Many Texians, believing the war was over, returned home. This would prove unwise. Santa Anna, humiliated by his army's defeat, vowed revenge. He would restore the honor of his country … and his family.

Santa Anna quickly assembled a new fighting force called the Mexican Army of Operations. Convinced of an easy victory, Santa Anna even transferred his presidential

Who Was Sam Houston?

By the time Sam Houston had been appointed commander in chief of the Texas army, he had already served as the attorney general in Nashville, Tennessee; a two-time congressman for the state of Tennessee; and the governor of that same state. After two years as governor of Tennessee, however, Houston—who was born on March 2, 1793—resigned from office. The precise reason for Houston's resignation is unknown.

Houston, who reportedly stood some six feet six inches tall, spent the next six years among the Cherokee in what is now Oklahoma. In 1832, Houston made his first visit to Texas in an unsuccessful attempt to secure a land grant for the Cherokee tribe. Three years later, Houston moved to Texas for good.

In addition to commanding the Texas army, Houston would be elected by a landslide to serve as the first president of the new Republic of Texas. (In fact, he held the presidency twice.) And, after the annexation of Texas by the United States, Houston would twice be elected to the US Senate.

Houston died at home in Huntsville, Texas, on July 26, 1863. He was seventy years old. The city of Houston, Texas, is named in his honor.

duties to a subordinate so he could personally lead this new army. In December of 1835, Santa Anna and his men set off, their sights set on Béxar. Santa Anna's army soon met up with Cos and his remaining forces. Together, they forged on. Progress was slow, however, and supplies were scarce. Worse, the weather turned. Snow fell as temperatures plummeted. Many men died. Still, Santa Anna and Cos pressed on, crossing into Texas on February 17.

The Provisional Government Dissolves

The provisional government—created with the best of intentions—quickly devolved into dysfunction. Half the General Council felt the government had done too much to promote independence, while the other half felt it had not done enough.

In December of 1835, the government became bogged down in a plan to attack Matamoros, a Mexican port on the Rio Grande near the Gulf of Mexico. The idea was to inspire other Mexican states to join the fight against Santa Anna. Also, the port, which pulled in an estimated $100,000 per month (more than $2 million in today's money), would give the provisional government a much-needed source of revenue. As an added bonus, with the port under its control, Texas would hold the Gulf of Mexico from Matamoros to New Orleans while at the same time neutralize a key staging ground for Mexican troops. And of course, it would give the members of the Texian Army—who were bored—something to do. Most of the remaining volunteers at Béxar withdrew and made for Matamoros. They left fewer than one hundred men at Béxar, under the command of Lieutenant Colonel James C. Neill.

Henry Smith, head of the provisional government, thought this plan was lunacy—and he said as much to the General Council. The General Council, in turn, impeached

Texas and the Mexican War

Smith. Eventually, members of the government grew weary of the constant infighting. Moreover, they were unclear on who, exactly, was in charge. In time, they simply stopped appearing at meetings. By the end of January, the provisional government was essentially kaput. A new convention would not gather until March.

The Battle of the Alamo

Left with fewer than one hundred men, Lieutenant Colonel James C. Neill quickly called for reinforcements. Some came, but not many. When the armies of Santa Anna and Cos arrived in Béxar on February 23, the Texians were outmanned, outgunned, and completely unprepared. They quickly gathered what food they could and retreated to the Alamo mission just outside town.

For nearly two weeks, Mexican troops besieged the mission. The Texians again called for reinforcements. Lieutenant Colonel William Barret Travis sent a letter by messenger to convey the men's desperate situation. "I am besieged, by a thousand or more of the Mexicans under Santa Anna—I have sustained a continual Bombardment & cannonade for 24 hours & have not lost a man," wrote Travis. He continued, "The enemy has demanded a surrender at discretion, otherwise, the garrison are to be put to the sword, if the fort is taken—I have answered the demand with a cannon shot, & our flag still waves proudly from the walls." Travis added, "I shall never surrender or retreat." He then called for aid "with all dispatch," noting that the enemy was "receiving reinforcements daily." Travis closed by noting that if his call for aid went unheeded, "I am determined to sustain myself as long as possible & die like a soldier who never forgets what is due to his own honor & that of his country—Victory or Death."

The Legend of Davy Crockett

One soldier who was slain at the Alamo was American folk legend Davy Crockett. Crockett, born in Tennessee in 1786, had enjoyed great renown thanks to his exploits as both a frontiersman and a politician.

At the age of thirteen, Crockett, having "whupped the tar" out of a bully at school and fearing the inevitable punishment, ran away from home. He spent the next three years wandering the countryside. The skills he developed there no doubt came in handy when, in 1813, Crockett joined the local militia as a scout. For two years, he fought in the Creek War against the Creek people in Alabama.

His enlistment period over, Crockett returned to Tennessee. There, he served as a member of the Tennessee State House of Representatives and, later, in the US Congress. In 1835, disillusioned with politics, Crockett joined the fight in the Texas Revolution.

The specifics of his death at the Alamo are unknown. But one witness stated that Crockett and his comrades died "without complaining and without humiliating themselves before their torturers."

Alas, Travis's call for aid would indeed go largely unheeded. On March 6, Santa Anna's troops, flush with reinforcements, increased its attacks. Soon, they breached the walls of the mission. Some eighty Texians attempted to flee but were quickly slain by Mexican cavalry. Within an hour, the remaining Texians had been slaughtered.

The Goliad Campaign

As Santa Anna and Cos made for Béxar, a second contingent of the Mexican Army of Operations—this one led by General José de Urrea—headed for Matamoros. On February 27, they launched a surprise attack on Texian troops camped nearby, essentially wiping them out. A week later, the men launched an attack on another group of Texian troops, with the same result. The now-defunct provisional government's attempt to take the port at Matamoros was officially a failure.

Urrea's men marched on, now bound for Goliad, where, in October of 1835, settlers had stormed a Mexican garrison. On March 14, they arrived in Refugio, about 25 miles (40 km) south of their destination. There, they found a town in chaos. It had been ransacked the week before by Tejano fighters who supported Santa Anna. Also present were twenty-eight Texian troops, led by Captain Amon B. King, who had been summoned by townsfolk to evacuate pro-independence residents.

Upon learning of the Mexican army's arrival, King's men quickly barricaded themselves in the mission inside the town. Soon, some two hundred Texian reinforcements arrived, led by William Ward. However, a dispute over who was in charge—King or Ward—prompted King and his men to abandon the mission. Eventually, they were forced to surrender to Mexican troops. On March 16, most of the men, including King, were executed.

For their part, Ward's men continued their efforts to hold their position—and for a time, it worked. Soon, however, their fate became clear. Running low on supplies and ammunition, they retreated. Most made it almost as far as Victoria, where they were to join with Ward's commander, James Fannin, and his men. But by then, Victoria, too, had been overrun by Mexican troops. Fannin and his men were taken prisoner. Days later, Ward and his fighters would meet the same fate.

Although their captors had told Fannin, Ward, and their men that they would be deported to the United States, the Mexican army had other plans. On March 27, 1836, the prisoners—342 in all—were shot dead.

The Texas Convention of 1836

March of 1836 marked one more significant development in the Texas Revolution: the Texas Convention of 1836. During this meeting, delegates passed a number of important measures. Chief among these was the Texas Declaration of Independence, similar to that of the United States. It passed by a landslide on March 2.

In addition, the convention drafted and adopted a constitution, also similar to that of the United States. It described a similar government structure, consisting of a chief executive, a **bicameral** legislature, and a supreme court. Unlike its United States counterpart, however, the Texas Constitution expressly permitted slavery. Finally, the convention elected a president—David G. Burnet—and other key officers.

The Tide Turns

Spurred by defeats and by the advancing Mexican army, the tattered remnants of the Texian Army, led by Sam Houston, beat a hasty retreat. Houston knew that due to

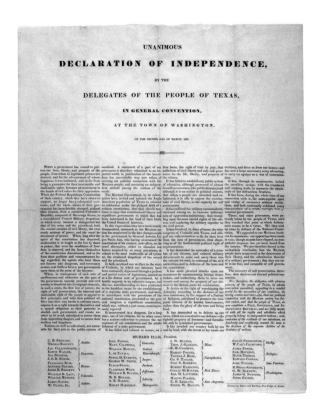

The Texas Declaration of Independence. Although based on the US Declaration of Independence, this document expressly permitted slavery.

losses sustained at the Alamo and Goliad, his men were the Texians' last hope. But he also knew that his men, many of whom were new volunteers, were ill-prepared for battle. They needed training—and fast. On March 28, after marching some 120 miles (193 km), Houston set up camp near San Felipe. There, in addition to taking some much-needed rest, the men practiced military drills.

Still, the Mexican army continued its relentless advance. Its target: the new provisional government, whose members were holed up in Harrisburg, Texas. On April 14, Santa Anna entered the town, only to find that government officials had fled to Galveston Island. Frustrated, he ordered that Harrisburg be torched.

By then, Houston's army, restored, sufficiently trained, and now in possession of two cannons provided by the

United States, was again on the move, marching for Harrisburg. The men arrived shortly after the departure of Mexican forces to find that all but one residence had burned to the ground. The same day, Texian forces captured a Mexican courier carrying intelligence on Mexican troops—including their numbers, location, and future plans. Emboldened, Houston prepared his men for attack.

The Battle of San Jacinto

On April 20, Houston and his troops—900 men—made camp in the Buffalo Bayou, near present-day Houston. Santa Anna's army arrived in the area soon thereafter. Santa Anna was quickly joined by reinforcements, led by Cos. The Mexican force was 1,200 men strong.

Houston chose his camp carefully. It provided excellent cover, enabling him to obscure his true numbers. Santa Anna was less shrewd, opting for a grassy plain bordered by woods on one side and a marsh and lake on the other.

On the morning of April 21, Mexican troops—exhausted after weeks of marching and perhaps underestimating their enemy—relaxed. That afternoon, the Texians made their move. After quietly dragging one of the cannons into position, they quickly fired several shots. Next, they fired what one witness described as their "first and last volley." Then the men swarmed the Mexican camp. "Remember the Alamo!" they cried. As one soldier recalled, "In a second we were into them with guns, pistols, and bowie knives."

The Mexican forces were taken quite by surprise. After just eighteen minutes, they abandoned camp, fleeing for their lives. "The entire enemy line, panic struck, took to flight," recalled one Texian soldier. In an attempt to escape, some Mexican soldiers splashed across the marsh toward the lake. Others made for the forest. But like Santa Anna

The Battle of San Jacinto. This was the deciding battle of the Texas Revolution.

at the Alamo, the Texians showed no mercy. They shot the terrified Mexican troops as they ran. It was, in the words of historian William C. Davis, "one of the most one-sided victories in history." Some six hundred Mexican soldiers were killed. Hundreds more were captured—including Santa Anna and Cos. In contrast, just eleven Texian soldiers lost their lives.

In exchange for his life, Santa Anna signed the Treaty of Velasco. This called for the cessation of hostilities between Mexico and Texas and the immediate evacuation of Mexican troops. In a secret version of the treaty, Santa Anna made yet more promises. One was to persuade the Mexican government to formally recognize the Republic of Texas, with the Rio Grande serving as the border between the two countries.

Despite Santa Anna's assurances, Mexico refused to recognize the newly formed Republic of Texas. The conflict between the two nations was far from over!

The flag for the new Republic of Texas flies over the Alamo.

CHAPTER THREE

The Republic of Texas is Born

Texas declared its independence on March 2, 1836. But it wasn't until the stunning defeat of Santa Anna at San Jacinto in April of that same year that Texians—or Texans, as they were sometimes called—could truly call themselves free. At last, the Republic of Texas was born.

There were problems, however. Mexico refused to abide by the terms of the Treaty of Velasco, despite it having been signed by Santa Anna himself. Mexico also declined to recognize Texas as an independent state. Worse, Mexican authorities had ordered the continuation of its war with Texas, although no assault on Texas proved forthcoming. This was fortunate indeed for Texas, for if such an attack had occurred, the depleted Texas army would surely have been defeated. It was simply incapable of defending the new nation's border with Mexico. It proved equally incapable of defending against the frequent raids by local Natives—particularly the powerful Comanches.

One reason the Texas army was so weak was that the provisional government, formed in March of 1836, was sorely lacking in funds. The new nation's treasury was empty—Texas had quickly incurred a debt of more than $1 million (more than $212 million in today's money)—and its credit was poor. Still, members of the provisional government pressed on. Interim president David G. Burnet called for elections. Residents of Texas were asked to approve the constitution that had been drafted during the Texas Convention of 1836 and to authorize the Texas Congress to amend that constitution. Residents were also asked to elect a president. Finally, they were asked to vote on a third issue: whether Texas should seek annexation with the United States—in other words, whether Texas should be absorbed by America.

On September 5, 1836, citizens of the Republic of Texas voted in their first national election. They overwhelmingly approved the constitution, although they rejected the idea that the Texas Congress should have the right to amend it. They also voted to pursue annexation. Finally, they chose Sam Houston as their president. Houston, whose name had become known far and wide during the Texas Revolution, won in a landslide, defeating Henry Smith and Stephen Austin. Mirabeau Lamar, who had fought alongside Houston in the Texas Revolution, was voted in as vice president.

The First Texas Congress

On October 3, 1836, the First Texas Congress—consisting of fourteen senators and twenty-nine representatives—convened in Columbia, Texas. Later that month, Houston took the oath of office. He then asked the senate to confirm his cabinet appointments. He named his rivals in the presidential election, Stephen Austin and Henry Smith, as secretary of state and secretary of the treasury, respectively. (Sadly, Austin would die of pneumonia just two months

Texas and the Mexican War

The Republic of Texas adopted the Lone Star as its flag. Today, the Lone Star serves as Texas's state flag.

later. He was forty-three years old. Upon learning of Austin's death, Houston proclaimed, "The Father of Texas is no more; the first pioneer of the wilderness has departed.")

Soon, the Texas Congress introduced a system of courts. This included a supreme court, with a chief justice appointed by the president and four associated justices who were elected by the state congress. In addition, county courts were established, with each court consisting of a chief justice and two associates. Each county was also allotted a sheriff, coroner, justices of the peace, and constables.

The Texas Congress quickly adopted a flag for the new nation. This flag had "an azure ground, with a large golden star central." Later, this flag would be replaced with the Lone Star flag. It features a blue vertical stripe on its left side and two horizontal stripes—one red and one white—on the right, with a lone white star in the center. The Lone Star flag remains in use today.

Choosing a national capital proved problematic. Some wanted Nacogdoches to serve as the capital. Others favored a site near wher the Battle of San Jacinto had been fought. In November of 1836, the Congress approved a temporary location: Houston, a new town under construction near Buffalo Bayou. In 1839, lawmakers selected a new site on the east bank of the Colorado River. This site, which they named Austin in honor of Stephen Austin, became the new capital of Texas.

Finally, the Texas Congress set the boundaries of the republic. The Rio Grande was the obvious choice for the southern border. Where to draw the eastern border with Louisiana was less clear. The matter would remain unresolved for some time. Indeed, this boundary would not be established until Texas was annexed by the United States more than ten years later.

Seeking Recognition by the United States

Even before the end of the Texas Revolution, the provisional government had sent representatives to the United States to seek recognition of Texas as an independent state. After the war, yet more agents were sent to ask the United States to intervene with Mexico to end hostilities and to convey Texas's interest in annexation.

The Americans were wary. Texas simply did not seem like a good bet. Its government was deep in debt. Moreover, in the words of US President Andrew Jackson, Texas was threatened by "an immense disparity of physical force on the side of Mexico." As noted by the Texas State Historical Association, "Texas independence was far from secure." And so, the United States initially opted against recognizing Texas or pursuing annexation.

Soon, however, the Americans changed their minds— at least on the issue of formally recognizing Texas. This was thanks to Powhatan Ellis, the US *charge d'affaires* (a person who takes the place of an ambassador when the ambassador is away) for Mexico. Ellis, fresh from a trip to Mexico City, informed his superiors that Mexico had descended into anarchy. In Ellis's view, a Mexican invasion of Texas was highly unlikely. In March of 1837, in his last act as president of the United States, President Jackson formally recognized Texas as an independent state—although he left the matter of annexation unresolved. France and England soon followed suit.

Mexico, however, continued to withhold acknowledgment of Texas's independence. Worse, Mexico continued to harass its neighbor to the north. In March of 1842, Mexico even went so far as to invade the young republic, briefly holding the city of San Antonio later that year.

The Push for Annexation

Soon after its inception, the Republic of Texas submitted a proposal for annexation to the United States. Why? First, Mexico remained a threat. Not only had Mexico refused to recognize the Republic of Texas, it had ceased to concede that the Texas Revolution was over. And of course, the Texas government—already deep in debt—lacked the funds to maintain a standing army. It simply did not have the means to secure its border. Second, the vast majority of settlers living in Texas had emigrated from the United States and continued to identify with their homeland.

As mentioned, the United States government rejected the proposal. The US government feared provoking a war with Mexico. But there was another reason: the anti-slavery abolitionist movement was steadily growing in the north. Its members did not wish to add a pro-slavery state—which Texas clearly was—to the Union. So, in October of 1838,

President Houston withdrew the proposal. For the time being, annexation was off the table.

By 1843, the mood in the United States had shifted. This was in part a response to views held by America's old adversary, Great Britain. The British opposed the annexation of Texas for three main reasons. First, it wanted to prevent the westward expansion of the United States. Second, it wanted to secure trade with Texas. And third, it opposed the institution of slavery and did not wish for it to expand in the United States. Indeed, Great Britain was so opposed to the annexation of Texas, it even considered the use of force to prevent it—although it did not carry out this plan. From the point of view of the United States, the more Great Britain worked to prevent annexation, the more attractive annexation became.

In April of 1844, US President John Tyler, who had assumed the office of the presidency after the untimely death of President William Henry Harrison, reopened talks on annexation. Tyler wasn't merely pro-annexation. In the words of historian Edward Crapol, the acquisition of Texas became "the primary objective of his administration." This was, in large part, due to Tyler's pro-slavery views.

Tyler sent representatives to negotiate a treaty with Texas. According to the terms of the treaty, the United States would admit Texas as a territory and assume its debt. Although most Texans preferred statehood to territorial status, they agreed to the terms. But when the issue went to ballot in the US Senate, it fell far short of the two-thirds majority it needed in order to pass.

Still, annexation remained an important issue in the United States. This was due in part to the growing sentiment that it was America's right—indeed, its duty—to expand westward. This expansionist view came to be called "manifest destiny." It was on this platform that Democratic

President James K. Polk

presidential candidate James K. Polk ran in 1844. Throughout Polk's campaign, he called for the annexation of Texas. Polk also called for the annexation of Oregon, whose ownership at that time was unclear.

Polk won the election. In Tyler's view, Polk's victory signified a mandate on the issue of annexation. On December 2, 1844, Tyler—still in office— urged Congress to pass a **joint resolution** on the matter. On February 28, 1845, Congress obliged. This time, the terms were more generous, calling for the annexation of Texas as a state rather than a territory. The United States would also take over dealings with Mexico. Tyler signed the resolution on March 1, 1845, just two days before leaving office.

Of course, Texas had to agree to the terms. But there was a rub: Mexico was ready to deal. Mexico promised to recognize the Republic of Texas, but only if it remained an independent state. Which offer should Texas accept— annexation or independence? In July of 1845, Texas lawmakers voted to adopt the US joint resolution and to reject Mexico's offer of recognition. They also drafted a new state constitution that, like its predecessor, explicitly permitted slavery. In October of that same year, Texas voters ratified the constitution by an overwhelming majority. In December, US president James K. Polk

The Republic of Texas is Born

Manifest Destiny

In 1811, John Quincy Adams, who would later become president of the United States, wrote, "The whole continent of North America appears to be destined by Divine Providence to be peopled by one nation, speaking one language, professing one general system of religious and political principles, and accustomed to one general tenor of social usages and customs." This view, referred to as continentalism, quickly gained traction among Americans.

In 1845, John L. O'Sullivan, the editor of an influential magazine, coined a new term to describe this view: manifest destiny. He wrote that it was "the fulfillment of our manifest destiny to overspread the continent allotted by Providence for the free development of our yearly multiplying millions." O'Sullivan used the phrase again later that same year, noting that the United States should be free to claim "the whole of Oregon ... by the right of our manifest destiny to overspread and to possess the whole of the continent which Providence has given us for the development of the great experiment of liberty and federated self-government entrusted to us."

Inherent in this view were two key points. First, the American people and their institutions held special virtues. (This is often referred to—even today—as American exceptionalism.) Second, it was both the destiny and the duty of the United States to remake the American West in its own image. Simply put, according to author

Reginald Horsman, Americans believed themselves to be "innately superior" and "destined to bring good government, commercial prosperity and Christianity to the American continents and the world."

Not everyone held these views, however. Massachusetts Representative Robert Winthrop wryly noted, "I suppose the right of manifest destiny to spread will not be admitted to exist in any nation except the universal Yankee nation." Nevertheless, the notion of manifest destiny took root. The United States would indeed spread.

Of course, spreading often meant encroaching on lands that were already held by Native people. This did not give the Americans pause. As noted by Horsman, manifest destiny held that these Native people "were doomed to subordinate status or extinction." Indeed, thanks to manifest destiny, several groups of Native people were simply killed. Others were force to settle in Indian Territory (what is now Oklahoma).

Eventually, the notion of manifest destiny would evolve to include overseas expansion, as evidenced by the annexation of the Republic of Hawaii in 1898. "It is manifest destiny," President William McKinley said of the move. (Others referred to this as plain old imperialism.) Later, the phrase "manifest destiny" would be used to describe America's belief that it is obligated to promote and preserve democracy abroad—a belief many Americans still hold today.

signed the Texas Admission Act into law. Texans elected a governor—J. Pinckney Henderson, who had been instrumental in the drive for annexation—and other state officials. On February 19, 1846, a ceremony in Austin marked the formal transfer of authority. "The final act in this great drama is now performed," said Anson Jones, who had been elected president of the Texas Republic in 1844. "The Republic of Texas is no more." Now, it was the twenty-eighth state in the Union.

Trouble with Mexico

Mexico was ready to deal with Texas if it remained an independent state. After annexation, however, that was no longer the case. Not only did Mexico refuse to recognize that Texas was part of the Union, claiming that Texas belonged to Mexico, it severed all diplomatic ties with the United States.

The United States sought to secure the border between Texas and Mexico. The border's precise location, however, remained in dispute. According to the Treaty of Velasco, which marked the end of the Texas Revolution, the border was the Rio Grande. But Mexico, which refused to acknowledge the treaty, claimed the border was the Nueces River, some 150 miles (241 km) to the north.

In July of 1845, President Polk sent troops to Texas to settle the dispute. Led by General Zachary Taylor, this fighting force of some 3,500 men marched for the Rio Grande. There, they constructed a fort opposite the Mexican city of Matamoros. They called it Fort Texas.

Polk also attempted a diplomatic solution. In November of 1845, he sent a representative to Mexico City to offer $25 million (more than $626 million in today's money) to the Mexican government. In exchange, Polk wanted the disputed territory between the Nueces River and the Rio

UNITED STATES

Arkansas R.

Claimed

Territory

Rio
Grande

TEXAS

Washington

S. Antonio

Nueces River

MEXICO

This map shows the disputed territory along the Texas-Mexico border.

Grande as well as the Mexican provinces of Alta California (a region that now includes the states of California, Arizona, and Nevada) and Nuevo Mexico (which included most of present-day New Mexico as well as parts of Texas, Colorado, Wyoming, Kansas, and Oklahoma). Mexico rejected the offer. In its view, selling these territories would be an affront

The Mexican-American War: A Mexican Perspective

The Mexican people questioned the United States' rationale. Many Mexicans believed—correctly, it would seem—that the American government was more interested in claiming new territory than defending what they already owned. The Mexicans viewed the Mexican-American War, which they called the US Invasion of Mexico or the US War Against Mexico—as offensive in nature. As noted in *El Republicano*, a Mexican newspaper, "No one has any doubts about the intentions the Washington cabinet has had for some time now with respect to Mexico ... One fights in the name of usurpation; the other defends justice."

This notion is supported by the fact that Mexico never itself declared war against the United States. Rather, it passed a Congressional decree in July of 1846 containing this key article: "The government, in the natural defense of the nation, will repel the aggression initiated and sustained by the United States of America against the Republic of Mexico, having invaded and committed hostilities in a number of the departments making up Mexican territory."

Once the war had begun, Mexico believed it was in no position to accept any peace offered by the United States. As written in 1847 in another Mexican newspaper, *El Diario del Gobierno*: "[The peace] that now could be accorded between the Mexican Republic and that of North America, would be humiliating to the first, and would gain to her, in the years to come, a dishonor among the rest of the nations, as well as domestic evils of such magnitude, that Mexico soon would be again theater of war and would disappear from the catalogue of the free and independent peoples." Mexican historian Jesús Velasco-Márquez put it this way: "During the entire conflict ... Mexico defended its territory and if at any time its position was belligerent, it was belligerent in the defense of national security and for the preservation of international legal order." Velasco-Márquez continued: "It was not a result of arrogance, nor of irresponsibility, but rather the only possible response to the arguments and the actions of the US government."

to the nation's honor. But in truth, even if the Mexican government *had* wanted to sell these territories, it likely would have been unable to do so due to its instability—in 1846, the presidency changed hands an astonishing four times. The War Ministry and Finance Ministry were even more unstable, being placed under new management six and sixteen times, respectively.

Shots Fired

On April 25, 1846, Mexican cavalry attacked a US patrol in the disputed territory between the Nueces River and the Rio Grande, killing sixteen men. For President Polk, this incident—dubbed the Thornton Affair, after the patrol's commanding officer—along with Mexico's refusal to sell its territory to the United States, was cause for war.

On May 11, Polk brought the case for war to Congress. "The cup of forbearance has been exhausted, even before Mexico passed the boundary of the United States, invaded our territory, and shed American blood upon American soil," Polk said.

Some opposed the action, viewing it as nothing more than a grab for territory. Joshua Giddings, a Democrat from Ohio, called it "an aggressive, unholy, and unjust war." He went on to say, "In the murder of Mexicans upon their own soil, or in robbing them of their country, I can take no part either now or hereafter." Another dissenter, Abraham Lincoln, demanded to know precisely where Thornton's men had been attacked, questioning whether it was indeed on American soil. And Whig leader Robert Toombs of Georgia said, "We charge the president with usurping the war-making power … with seizing a country … which had been for centuries, and was then in the possession of the Mexicans." He implored, "Let us put a check upon this lust of dominion.

Texas and the Mexican War

We had territory enough, Heaven knew." Still, just two days after Polk's address, Congress voted to declare war.

For all practical purposes, however, the fighting had already commenced. On May 3, Mexican troops at Matamoros opened fire on Fort Texas. Soldiers at Fort Texas fired back. For six days, the siege of Fort Texas continued. Slowly, Mexican forces encircled the fort. Still, the Americans held firm. On May 6, Mexican General Mariano Arista demanded their surrender. Captain Edgar S. Hawkins—who had assumed command of the fort when his superior, Major Jacob Brown, was mortally wounded—responded, "My interpreter is not skilled in your language but if I understand you correctly … I must respectfully decline to surrender." (The fort would later be renamed Fort Brown, after the fallen major.)

Soon, the Americans received a reprieve. Aware that American reinforcements were en route, Arista moved his army to block them. On May 8, Arista's army met these reinforcements—led by General Taylor, who, after building Fort Texas, had been stationed near Corpus Christi—at nearby Palo Alto. There, Mexican forces quickly fell to the Americans' flying artillery. Those Mexican soldiers who survived quickly retreated to a more defensible position along a nearby riverbed, called the Resaca de la Palma.

The next day, Mexican and American troops engaged in vicious hand-to-hand combat along the riverbed. Soon, the US cavalry captured the Mexican artillery, including two 8-pounder bronze guns, two 6-pounder bronze guns, and four 4-pounder bronze guns. The Mexicans, aware they had been beaten, fled in panic. Leaving their baggage behind, including General Arista's writing desk and silver service, soldiers attempted to swim to safety across the Rio Grande. Many drowned.

The Mexican-American War had begun.

General Scott and his troops enter Mexico City during the Mexican-American War.

CHAPTER FOUR

War with Mexico

On May 13, 1846, the United States declared war on Mexico. President Polk quickly outlined a four-pronged attack. The first two prongs centered on present-day California and New Mexico. The remaining two involved attacks into the heart of Mexico.

The California Campaign

Interestingly, American settlers in modern-day California, which was then part of a Mexican state called Alta California, took action against Mexico even before they learned that war had been declared.

On June 14, 1846, one month after Congress's declaration of war but several weeks before official word of that fact arrived in the region—there were no railways, steamships, or telegraph wires in the area—thirty-four American settlers in the Sacramento Valley seized control of Sonoma, an undefended Mexican outpost. This was in response to a rumor that General José Castro, the senior

Mexican military officer in Alta California, was gathering an army to expel the settlers from the area. By early July, the number of rebels would grow to nearly three hundred. One rebel designed a flag featuring the words "California Republic" beneath a star and a grizzly bear, which was hoisted over Sonoma. Thereafter, the rebels were called Bear Flaggers, and the land they occupied called the Bear Flag Republic.

On July 2, the Bear Flaggers took Yerba Buena (now called San Francisco). There, they joined forces with a group led by John C. Frémont. Frémont had been surveying the Oregon Territory. When he learned that war between the United States and Mexico was imminent, he and his party made for Alta California. Frémont's men, along with the Bear Flaggers, united to form the California Battalion. Still, official word about the declaration of war had not yet arrived. Frémont was not acting under military orders, but operating under his own authority.

California rebels designed this flag, which remains California's state flag.

Texas and the Mexican War

Around the same time, Commodore John D. Sloat, commander of the US Navy's Pacific Squadron, reached nearby Monterey, California by sea. He had been instructed to take the San Francisco Bay and to cordon off various Alta California ports when he was certain the war had begun. Sloat, assuming that Frémont was acting on orders from Washington, took Monterey on July 7. "Henceforth California would be a portion of the United States," he proclaimed. Two days later, Sloat's forces landed at Yerba Buena. The northern part of Alta California was under American control even before the official word on the declaration of war had arrived.

Soon, the southern part of Alta California would be as well. Commodore Robert F. Stockton, who assumed command of the Pacific Squadron on July 15, ordered Frémont and his men to San Diego. At the same time, Stockton sent 360 of his own men to nearby San Pedro. Both groups would then march to Los Angeles, which they would capture without resistance on August 13. For his part, General Castro, along with the Mexican governor of Alta California, Pío de Jesús Pico, fled the state. "California is entirely free from Mexican dominion," Stockton wrote to US Secretary of State James Buchanan.

Nuevo México and the Southwest

Two days after Frémont and Stockton captured Los Angeles, US Brigadier General Stephen W. Kearny, commander of the Army of the West, took Santa Fe—and, with it, the entire Mexican territory of Nuevo México—without firing a single shot. In the face of the oncoming American troops, Nuevo México Governor Manuel Armijo retreated to Chihuahua, 500 miles (805 km) to the south.

With Nuevo México subdued, Kearny divided his forces. About eight hundred of his men remained in Santa Fe. Another eight hundred men were ordered to capture El Paso. Kearny led a third group—this one numbering some three hundred men—to Alta California, setting out on September 25, 1846.

Along the way, Kearny encountered famous frontiersman Kit Carson, who shared the news of victory in Alta California. Relieved, Kearny sent two hundred of his men back to Santa Fe. He also asked Carson to serve as his guide. Carson agreed. Together, Kearny, Carson, and the remaining men pushed on toward the Pacific.

What Kearny and Carson didn't know was that on September 29, a group of **Californios** had attacked the garrison at Los Angeles and forced the Americans out. These same Californios—who acted alone, without the aid of the Mexican government—also recaptured garrisons in San Diego and Santa Barbara.

Clearly, Kearny and Carson would not enter Los Angeles unopposed. On December 6, they encountered a group of Californios in the San Pasqual Valley, some 28 miles (45 km) from San Diego. Kearny's men were at a distinct disadvantage for several reasons. First, the Californios, led by Major Andrés Pico—brother of former Mexican governor Pío Pico—knew the terrain. Second, their horses were fresh. And third, the weather was damp. As a result, the Americans lost the ability to use their gunpowder, which had grown soggy. Their weapons, carbines and pistols, were rendered useless against the long lances favored by the Californios.

The next day, Kearny's men, of whom seventeen had been killed and eighteen wounded, including Kearny himself, rallied to establish a defensive position. Aiding in their efforts was the fact that the weather had turned, allowing their gunpowder to finally dry. That evening,

Famous frontiersman Kit Carson. Carson would serve as a guide to US Brigadier General Stephen W. Kearny en route from Nuevo México to Alta California.

Carson snuck across enemy lines to carry a request for reinforcements to Commodore Stockton, who was headquartered in nearby San Diego. Realizing his shoes made too much noise, Carson removed them. "Had to travel over a country covered with prickly pear and rocks, barefoot," Carson later stated in his memoirs. For his

Kit Carson

By the time Christopher "Kit" Carson met Brigadier General Kearny, he was already well-known thanks to John C. Frémont. Carson had served as a guide for Frémont as he explored Alta California, Oregon, and the Great Basin area. To encourage more Americans to move west, Frémont published accounts of his expeditions, in which Carson figured prominently.

Carson was born in 1809 in Kentucky, but his family soon moved to Missouri. As a young teenager, he became a saddler's apprentice in Franklin, Missouri, which marked the eastern end of the Santa Fe Trail. Carson was quickly dazzled by tales of the trail told by the trappers and traders who frequented the saddle shop. Soon, he decided to travel the trail himself, reaching Santa Fe in November of 1826. Carson settled in nearby Taos, where he learned the skills of a trapper. Carson also learned to speak fluent Spanish and even picked up several Native languages.

Starting in 1829, Carson embarked on various trapping expeditions, crisscrossing the American West. Often, these expeditions came under attack from local Native American tribes. He quickly developed a reputation as a good—if merciless—fighter. Later, Carson would engage in countless conflicts with Native Americans on behalf of the US government. Initially, Carson despised the Native people. In time, however, his views would shift. Indeed, Carson's first two wives were Native Americans.

Carson met Frémont in 1842. "I was pleased with him and his manner of address at this first meeting," Frémont later wrote. Frémont quickly offered Carson, whom he described as "a man of medium height, broad-shouldered, and deep-chested, with a clear steady blue eye and frank speech and address; quiet and unassuming," a job as a guide, paying $100 per month—a veritable fortune to Carson. Between 1842 and 1845, Carson and Frémont mapped terrain along the Oregon Trail to the Columbia River in Oregon.

Somehow, Carson again found time to wed again in 1843, marrying a young Mexican woman, Josefa Jaramillo. Together, they would have eight children.

In time, Carson, who later fought in the Civil War on the side of the north, would become a legend of sorts. Fictionalized accounts of his adventures began to appear. In 1856, Carson attempted to set the record straight by dictating his life story to a scribe. For many years, Americans viewed Carson as a hero. Eventually, however, a different narrative emerged: Carson was seen as a "butcher" of Native Americans. One journalist, Virginia Hopkins, wrote that "Kit Carson was directly or indirectly responsible for the deaths of thousands of Indians."

In 1863, Carson's wife Josefa died. Grief-stricken, Carson himself died a month later, on May 23, at the age of fifty-eight.

part, Stockton quickly obliged, dispatching more than two hundred men to the San Pasqual valley. The Battle of San Pasqual was effectively over. The Californios dispersed, leaving Stockton's men to escort Kearny's bedraggled troops to San Diego, where they arrived on December 12.

On December 29, after some much-needed rest, Kearny led a force of six hundred men to Los Angeles, 150 miles (241 km) away. On January 8, near the San Gabriel River, they encountered an army of Californios led by General José María Flores. Kearny himself described the ensuing Battle of Rio San Gabriel as follows:

> We proceeded on our route without seeing the enemy till the 8th instant, when they showed themselves in full force of six hundred mounted men, with four pieces of artillery, under their Governor Flores, occupying the heights in front of us, which commanded the crossing of the river San Gabriel, and they ready to oppose our further progress. The necessary disposition of our troops was immediately made, by covering our front with a strong party of skirmishers, placing our wagons and baggage train in rear of them, and protecting the flanks and rear with the remainder of the command. We then proceeded, forded the river, carried the heights, and drove the enemy from them after an action of about one and a half hours, during which they made a charge upon our left flank, which was repulsed; soon after which, they retreated and left us in possession of the field, on which we encamped that night.

Kearny continued:

Texas and the Mexican War

The next day, the 9th instant, we proceeded on our march at the usual hour, the enemy in front and on our flanks, and when we reached the plains of the Mesa, their artillery again opened upon us, when their fire was returned by our guns as we advanced; and after hovering around and near us for about two hours, occasionally skirmishing with us during that time, they concentrated their force and made another charge on our left flank, which was quickly repulsed; shortly after which they retired, we continuing our march; and in the afternoon encamped on the bank of the San Fernando, three miles below this city, which we entered the following morning without molestation.

Kearny had recaptured Los Angeles. Shortly thereafter, he was joined by Frémont, whose army had taken Santa Barbara on December 27. United States forces now held all of Alta California.

On January 13, Frémont and Andrés Pico signed the Treaty of Cahuenga. Although this treaty was in fact unofficial—it did not have the backing of the US or Mexican government—it effectively terminated all fighting in Alta California.

General Taylor Takes Monterrey and Saltillo

As Frémont, Stockton, and Kearny worked to take Nuevo México and Alta California, others turned southward, toward the heart of Mexico. Among these was General Zachary Taylor. Taylor, whose father had fought in the American Revolution, had himself enjoyed a long and

The Rise and Fall of Antonio López de Santa Anna

Antonio López de Santa Anna was nothing if not a survivor. After his defeat at the hands of the Texians in the Texas Revolution, Santa Anna was exiled to the United States. Finally, in 1837, Mexico permitted his return. He settled in Veracruz.

In 1838, Santa Anna saw his chance for redemption. That year, French forces invaded Veracruz. Santa Anna petitioned for and was granted control of the army, with orders to expel the French. During the ensuing fighting, Santa Anna was struck in the leg by cannon fire. There was no choice but to amputate. (Santa Anna ordered that his leg be buried with full military honors.) Although Santa Anna's efforts against the French were ultimately unsuccessful, the Mexican people nonetheless viewed him as a hero. This allowed him to achieve his true goal: a return to politics.

Mexico was in disarray. The current president, Anastasio Bustamante, had lost his grip on the nation. Supporters urged Santa Anna to take charge. Once again, Santa Anna became president of Mexico.

This proved problematic. Mexico was broke. To restore the treasury, Santa Anna sought to raise taxes. Several Mexican states responded by severing ties with Santa

Anna's government. Two states went even further, declaring themselves independent republics. Santa Anna's increasingly autocratic leadership style turned even his friends against him. In 1844, fearing assassination, Santa Anna fled. He was captured early the next year and exiled to Cuba.

Santa Anna was down, but not out. In August of 1846, after the outbreak of the Mexican-American War, Santa Anna offered his services to US president James K. Polk to help bring about peace. According to historians Larry Schweikart and Michael Allen, "Polk negotiated a deal to not only bring Santa Anna back [to Mexico], but to pay him $2 million—ostensibly a bribe as an advance payment on the cession of California." Not surprisingly, when Santa Anna returned to Mexico, he quickly went back on his offer to Polk, offering his services to the Mexican president. After being appointed commanding general of the Mexican forces, Santa Anna then seized the presidency for himself.

Once again, his reign would be short. In 1848, following the Mexican-American War, Santa Anna was again exiled, this time to Jamaica. Five years later, in 1853, supporters helped him to again take the Mexican presidency. In 1855, he was exiled for the last time, this time for good. The government tried him for treason *in absentia* and seized his estates. Eventually, in 1874, Santa Anna was permitted to return. Old and infirm, he was no longer a threat to the Mexican government. He died two years later in Mexico City. He was eighty-two years old.

General Zachary Taylor, who would later be elected president of the United States

honorable career in the US Army. After defeating Mexican forces at the Battle of Palo Alto and the Battle of Resaca de la Palma in May of 1846, he relieved forces at Fort Texas. From there, on the orders of President Polk, General Taylor—often called "Old Rough and Ready" due to his direct demeanor, fearless nature, and willingness to endure hardships in the field—crossed the Rio Grande to occupy Metamoros, where he remained until August. Flush with fresh troops, Taylor then marched to Monterrey, Mexico, arriving on September 19. Two days later, Taylor attacked the city. Although he sustained heavy losses—450 of his men were killed—Taylor ultimately prevailed, capturing Monterrey. Rather than pushing for full-scale surrender, however, Taylor accepted a truce that many, including President Polk, saw as too liberal.

Incensed, Polk ordered the bulk of Taylor's forces to join General Winfield Scott, who was planning a campaign to take Mexico City. Taylor then marched with his greatly diminished army to Saltillo. There, they set up camp on a mountain pass called Buena Vista. Antonio López de Santa Anna, who had so bedeviled the Texans during the Texas Revolution and had since reclaimed the Mexican presidency, was determined to strike Taylor while he was vulnerable. Leading an army of twenty thousand men, Santa Anna personally marched north from Mexico City to Buena Vista. Upon his arrival on February 22, 1847, he demanded Taylor's immediate surrender. Taylor, though greatly outnumbered, declined. The next day, Santa Anna attacked.

Initially, signs were favorable for Santa Anna. His men quickly flanked the US troops and inflicted considerable casualties. Still, the Americans held firm, routing a Mexican cavalry as it attempted to break through their lines. By the end of the day, the Americans, 650 of whom would perish in the battle, had killed or wounded more than 3,400 Mexican troops. The next day, Santa Anna, having received word of upheaval in Mexico City, withdrew. Although he declared victory, he had in fact left Taylor—who, in 1848, would be elected president of the United States, thanks in large part to his military record—in control of the area.

General Scott Marches on Mexico City

As mentioned, the bulk of General Taylor's forces were ordered to transfer to General Winfield Scott's command. Like Taylor, Scott was a longtime army man. He had even earned a Congressional gold medal for his service during the War of 1812. Thanks to his reputation for imposing strict discipline, he had also earned an unfortunate nickname: "Old Fuss and Feathers."

Although Scott was strongly opposed to President Polk's policies toward Mexico, he had proposed a bold plan for victory. This involved sailing to Veracruz, Mexico, a city founded by Hernán Cortés himself, and from there marching on to Mexico City. Polk, who had punished Scott for his outspoken views by denying him command of the army during the conflict, grudgingly agreed to the plan.

Life in the US Army

During the course of the Mexican-American War, the US army grew from just over 6,000 men to more than 115,000. Many joined the army for the opportunities it would provide. Most did not realize, however, just how difficult army life would be.

For one, the food was terrible. According to historian James M. McCaffrey, "The soldier's basic ration consisted of beef or pork, hard bread (or flour or cornmeal with which to bake bread), peas, beans, or rice, and a little salt, sugar, and coffee as available." For another, the housing was basic at best. As McCaffrey notes, "These simple affairs, each designed to accommodate six men and their bedrolls, offered far less protection against the wind and rain than even the rudest log cabins back home." Still, most soldiers likely preferred life at camp to the long marches they were forced to undertake—while carrying some 30 pounds (13.6 kilograms) or more of gear.

Of course, these soldiers knew their lives would be put at risk while in battle. But in truth, they were far more likely to die of disease. McCaffrey writes, "Yellow fever, malaria, dysentery, smallpox, measles, and various other diseases prevalent in Mexico were a constant scourge to the US soldiers and killed far more than did Mexican bullets."

Perhaps all these factors explain why so many American soldiers—some 8.3 percent—deserted!

On March 9, 1847, Scott alit south of Veracruz. By March 12, his men had Veracruz, and the 3,400 Mexican troop members stationed there, surrounded. Scott's soldiers proceeded to build a series of earthworks and trenches to serve as protection. On March 21, after the arrival of a half-dozen heavy guns, Scott was ready. The next day, he attacked. On March 28, Mexican forces inside the city surrendered. Veracruz had fallen.

From Veracruz, which would serve as a vital supply base for US forces for the duration of the war, Scott marched westward toward Puebla, the second-largest city in Mexico. En route, he encountered the notorious Santa Anna, whose twelve thousand troops, fresh from their "win" in Buena Vista, lay in wait near Cerro Gordo. Fortunately for Scott, Santa Anna's men revealed their position prematurely. Scott was then able to reroute his troops to the north, quietly flanking the enemy. On April 18, the American forces routed their Mexican foes, taking possession of their artillery and supplies.

Scott pushed on to Puebla, arriving on May 1. Thanks to its citizens' intense dislike of President Santa Anna, Scott was able to take the city without firing a shot. Scott remained in Puebla for some months to gather supplies and reinforcements. Finally, on August 7, he marched on toward Mexico City.

On August 20, Scott's men won not one but two battles, in Contreras and Churubusco, on the outskirts of Mexico City. These victories were followed by a third on September 8 at the Battle of Molino del Rey, although this one came at a higher cost. Nearly one in four Americans in that battle perished. Still, however, entry into Mexico City eluded Scott.

Scott would finally claim victory just four days later when his troops overran Chapultepec, near the Molino del Rey. Just 2 miles (3.2 km) from the city walls, Chapultepec was

The storming of Chapultepec, a castle that served as an important defensive post for Mexico City

Texas and the Mexican War

a castle that had been converted to house the Mexican Military Academy. It was under the control of one General Nicolás Bravo, who had under his command fewer than one thousand men—including two hundred cadets, some of whom were just thirteen years old. On September 12, Scott's men stormed the castle. Bravo's forces fought valiantly, including the cadets. Even after Bravo ordered them to retreat, six of these cadets—boys between the ages of thirteen and nineteen—fought on to the death. (Forever after, these six would be known as *Los Niños Héroes*, or the Child Heroes.) But their efforts were in vain. By 9:00 a.m. the following morning, Bravo was forced to surrender. Santa Anna watched from afar as Scott's troops hoisted the American flag over the castle. He is said to have exclaimed, "I believe if we were to plant our batteries in Hell the damned Yankees would take them from us!"

All that was left was to enter the city, which Scott's men would do in short order later that same day. Although Scott did not technically hold the city—Santa Anna remained inside, bunkered in the Ciudedala, or citadel—he would soon enough. Early the next morning, Santa Anna ordered his men to retreat outside the city. City officials then called on Scott to inform him of their unconditional surrender. Mexico City had fallen. And although the war wasn't over yet, it would be soon.

The Treaty of Guadalupe Hidalgo. This treaty ended the Mexican-American war and ceded vast tracts of land to the United States.

CHAPTER FIVE

The Aftermath of War

On September 13, 1837, General Winfield Scott's troops overran Mexico City. Antonio López de Santa Anna, the president of Mexico, was forced to withdraw with his troops outside the city. The war wasn't over, but it was close. Before hostilities would cease, Santa Anna—who, in order to focus on the impending combat, surrendered the presidency—would make one more attempt to defeat the Americans.

Santa Anna sought to cut off Scott's supply route, which spanned from Veracruz to Mexico City. A key post on this route was the city of Puebla, which Scott had conquered the previous spring. Santa Anna believed that if he could retake Puebla, then guarded by some five hundred American soldiers, it might turn the war in Mexico's favor.

On the night of September 13, the same day Mexico City fell, one of Santa Anna's men, General Joaquín Rea, led an attack on Puebla. The Americans inside the city, who were split among a convent, Fort Loretto, and the Citadel of San José, held firm. On September 16, Rea demanded their surrender, but still the Americans remained. Even when Santa Anna himself arrived with some five hundred reinforcements on September 22, the Americans would not be moved.

On it went, until finally, at the end of September, Santa Anna blinked. Informed of incoming American reinforcements led by General Joseph Lane, Santa Anna abandoned Puebla and went on the attack against Lane. The two sides met on October 9 in Huamantla, some 25 miles (40 km) from Puebla. There, Santa Anna was soundly defeated. Lane and his troops marched on, arriving in Puebla on October 12, ending the siege—and, for all practical purposes, the war.

Once again, Santa Anna was down. No longer president, he was also asked by the new Mexican leader, Manuel de la Peña y Peña, to surrender command of the army. Once again, he was exiled, this time to Jamaica.

The Treaty of Guadalupe Hidalgo

Although the fighting had ceased with the conclusion of the Siege of Puebla and the Battle of Huamantla, the Mexican-American War was not officially over until February 2, 1848. On that day, representatives from the United States and Mexico signed the Treaty of Guadalupe. The US government ratified the treaty on March 10; Mexico followed suit on May 25.

Why did Mexico sign? For multiple reasons. First, it was outclassed militarily. It simply could not stand up to America's might. Second, many of its largest cities were occupied by American forces. Third, the country also faced many internal divisions.

The treaty did more than simply end the war. It also distributed the spoils. Specifically, the treaty ceded control

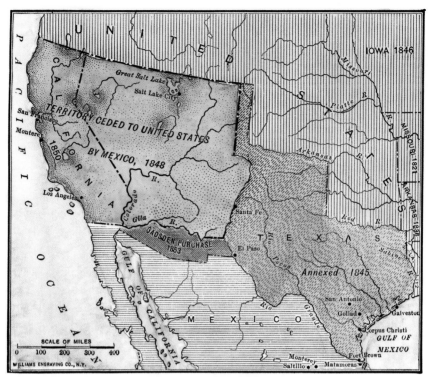

A map of the land ceded to the United States by Mexico

of Texas to the United States. It also turned over to the Americans the Mexican states of Nuevo México and Alta California, an area comprising modern-day California, Nevada, Utah, New Mexico, most of Arizona and Colorado, and parts of Texas, Oklahoma, Kansas, and Wyoming. In all, Mexico lost more than 500,000 square miles (1,294,994 sq km) of territory, more than half its land. The area, which became known as the Mexican Cession, was about the size of Europe. It was the third-largest acquisition of territory in American history, after the Louisiana Purchase and Alaska.

What did Mexico get for its trouble? Of course, US troops were withdrawn from Mexican territory. In addition, the United States paid Mexico a sum of $15 million (more than $400 million in today's money) for the land. It also waived some $3.25 million (nearly $90 million in today's money) in debts

The Role of Communications in the Mexican-American War

The United States gained a clear advantage over its foes through its use of communication. Thanks to several advancements in technology, communication could occur more quickly than ever before. In times past, news of events could take weeks or even months to travel. Now, all that was changing.

What advancements, specifically, had occurred? First was the invention of the river steamship in the early 1800s. As noted by author Donald S. Frazier, "This technological conquest of river currents allowed for relatively rapid transfer of materials and information both upstream and downstream, turning streams and waterways into natural highways." Second came the development of a railway system, which augmented communication efforts. Finally, and perhaps most importantly, was the invention of the telegraph in 1844, which enabled the transmission of messages across copper wires. Together, these three innovations "advanced critical communications at speeds before unimagined."

How did this advancement affect the outcome of the Mexican-American War? According to Frazier, "In the United States, news from the front arrived in just a few days, and politicians and generals alike could react rapidly to changing circumstances." As a result, "Materials and manpower arrived from remote locations in the United States at a steady and reliable pace." This made it possible for the United States "to conduct a foreign war far removed from its centers of population."

These advancements in communications also had a profound effect on the US press, which could report on developments in the field more quickly than ever before. For the first time in American history, journalists, rather than just politicians, could influence people's opinions and attitudes. And as Americans received more and more reports from the battlefield, they became emotionally invested in the war.

owed by Mexico to the United States. (In 1953, in a deal called the Gadsden Purchase, the United States purchased another 30,000 square miles, or 77,700 sq km, from Mexico, clearing the route for a transcontinental railroad.)

Not all Americans were happy with the terms of the treaty. Some felt like the United States didn't go far enough. Members of the so-called All Mexico Movement proposed that the United States take over *all* of Mexico's territories. Others felt the treaty had gone too far. One such person was Nicholas Trist, who signed the treaty on the behalf of the United States. After adding his signature, Trist is said to have told his wife, "Could those Mexicans have seen into my heart at that moment, they would have known that my feeling of shame as an American was far stronger than theirs could be as Mexicans." He continued, "For though it would not have done for me to say so there, that was a thing for every right minded American to be ashamed of, and I was ashamed of it, most cordially and intensely ashamed of it."

Famed US president and Civil War general Ulysses S. Grant, who served in the Mexican-American War under General Zachary Taylor, agreed. In his memoirs, published in 1885, Grant wrote, "I was bitterly opposed to the [the annexation of Texas], and to this day regard the war, which resulted, as one of the most unjust ever waged by a stronger against a weaker nation. It was an instance of a republic following the bad example of European monarchies, in not considering justice in their desire to acquire additional territory."

The Aftermath

According to historian David J. Weber, the Mexican-American War "made a profound difference in the United States' future shape—in our wealth with the discovery of gold in

Famed US president and Civil War general Ulysses S. Grant served under Zachary Taylor during the Mexican-American War, though he was opposed to the campaign.

California and in our image of ourselves as an expansionist, transcontinental empire, which later became a major player on the global stage." He continued, "The war certainly shaped the area in which many of us live today from Texas all the way to California." Weber goes on to note that, "for Mexicans, the reverse is certainly the case." In other words, everything that the United States gained, Mexico lost. "The war became a scar on the national psyche," Weber said.

Ultimately, the Mexican-American War, in the words of historian Antonia I. Castañeda, was primarily "about territory, continental expansion, access to the ports of the Pacific, and access to and ownership of all of the wonderful minerals and riches that were in the subsoil." In that regard, the United States was successful. After all, the primary effect of the Mexican-American War was the transfer of a significant amount of territory from Mexico to the United States.

According to Castañeda, however, territory wasn't the only thing at stake. The Mexican-American War was also "about slavery and access to more cotton-producing land that would increase the size of the slave population." Texas had been admitted to the Union as a slave state, and many in the US government sought to expand slavery even further.

In time, the Mexican-American War would be seen as an ugly precursor to the American Civil War, fought between the northern and southern American states over the issue of slavery. According to Ulysses S. Grant, "The Southern rebellion was largely the outgrowth of the Mexican war. Nations, like individuals, are punished for their transgressions. We got our punishment in the most sanguinary and expensive war of modern times."

Grant was just one of many military men who went from serving in the Mexican-American War to commanding forces in the American Civil War thirteen years later. Others included Robert E. Lee, Thomas "Stonewall" Jackson, and dozens more.

Writer Ralph Waldo Emerson put it this way: "The United States will conquer Mexico, but it will be as the man swallows the arsenic, which brings him down in turn. Mexico will poison us."

Even as late as 1880, the Mexican-American War continued to cast a dark shadow on American politics. That year, the Republican National Committee described the war as "feculent, reeking corruption." It went on to call it "one of the darkest scenes in our history—a war forced upon our and the Mexican people by the high-handed usurpations of Pres't Polk in pursuit of territorial aggrandizement of the slave oligarchy."

Another lasting effect of the Mexican-American War was the loss of civil and political rights experienced by

Latinos and Native Americans who remained in the annexed territories—despite assurances to the contrary in the Treaty of Guadalupe Hidalgo. Although the United States did grant American citizenship to Latinos in the area as promised, it withheld citizenship from Native Americans in the new territories until the 1930s, some ninety years later.

And of course, the war would have a tremendous impact on the relationship between the two nations involved. Historian Richard Griswold del Castillo notes, "Because of its military victory the United States virtually dictated the terms of settlement." In doing so, del Castillo argues, "The [Treaty of Guadalupe Hidalgo] established a pattern of political and military inequality between the two countries, and this lopsided relationship has stalked Mexican-US relations ever since." For Mexicans, says historian Robert Ryal Miller, the Mexican-American War "shattered a sense of national honor and dignity, and it engendered a deep and long-lasting feeling of resentment toward Yankees."

Regardless of which side one identifies with—the Mexicans or the Americans—as noted by historian Jesús Velasco-Márquez, "The war should leave us with a lesson for both countries, which is that geographically and historically we are intimately intertwined, and that we can affect each other greatly."

Chronology

1519 Spanish conquistadors land in Texas.

1685 French settlers land near Matagorda Bay.

1690 Spain builds its first mission in Texas, near present-day San Antonio.

1810 Mexican revolutionaries launch the Mexican War for Independence against Spain. Eleven years later, Mexico wins.

1821 Stephen F. Austin establishes a colony in Texas.

1835 Mexican President Antonio López de Santa Anna overturns Mexico's constitution.

October 1835 Residents in Gonzales, Texas, attack Mexican troops. The Texas Revolution begins.

March 2, 1836 Texas declares independence.

March 1836 Mexico wins the Battle of the Alamo. Later the same month, it defeats Texian forces near Goliad.

April 1836 Texas defeats Mexico at the Battle of San Jacinto. The Texas Revolution is effectively over.

September 5, 1836 The Republic of Texas holds its first election. Sam Houston is elected president.

1837 The United States, France, and England recognize Texas as an independent state. Mexico, however, refuses to do so.

1845 The United States annexes Texas.

April 25, 1846 Mexican cavalry attack a US patrol in disputed territory.

May 3, 1846 The Siege of Fort Texas on the Rio Grande begins. It ends on May 8, when American reinforcements arrive after winning the Battle of Palo Alto and the Battle of Resaca de la Palma.

May 13, 1846 The US Congress declares war against Mexico. The Mexican-American War begins.

June–July, 1846 Bear Flaggers seize Sonoma and Yerba Buena in Alta California. They then form the California Battalion with forces led by John C. Frémont.

July 7, 1846 The US Navy captures Monterey, California, and later lands at Yerba Buena. Northern Alta California is under American control.

August 13, 1846 American forces capture Los Angeles in Alta California.

August 15, 1846 US Brigadier General Stephen W. Kearny takes Nuevo México.

September 21, 1846 US General Zachary Taylor captures the Mexican city of Monterrey.

September 29, 1846 Californios capture the garrison at Los Angeles.

December 6, 1846 Kearny's men fight Californios in the San Pasqual Valley, near San Diego. They win the battle when reinforcements arrive two days later.

December 29, 1846 Kearny's forces recapture Los Angeles.

January 13, 1847 John C. Frémont and Mexican General Andrés Pico sign the Treaty of Cahuenga. This treaty, although unofficial, ends fighting in Alta California.

February 23, 1847 Taylor defeats Mexican forces at Buena Vista.

March 21, 1847 US troops led by General Winfield Scott capture Veracruz, Mexico.

May 1, 1847 Scott's forces take Puebla, Mexico's second-largest city.

August 20, 1847 The United States wins two battles, in Contreras and Churubusco, on the outskirts of Mexico City.

September 8, 1847 The United States wins the Battle of Molino del Rey.

September 13, 1847 US troops overrun Chapultepec, 2 miles (3.2 km) from Mexico City. Later that day, they enter the city.

September 13, 1847 The Siege of Puebla begins. It lasts until October 12, when American reinforcements arrive.

September 14, 1847 Mexico surrenders unconditionally, although the fighting is not over.

October 9, 1847 The United States defeats Mexico at the Battle of Huamantla, the last battle of the Mexican-American War.

February 2, 1848 The United States and Mexico sign the Treaty of Guadalupe, ending the Mexican-American War.

Glossary

abdicate To give up or renounce, as with a monarch renouncing his or her throne.

Amichel The name given by Spanish explorers to modern-day Texas.

Anglo The name given to settlers in Texas of European origin.

annex To absorb a territory.

assassinate The act of murdering another, typically an important person.

bicameral Describes a legislative body composed of two branches.

Californio The name given to Spanish-speaking people from Alta California.

colony An area under the control of another country and settled by people from that country.

conquistador A Spanish explorer.

delegate A person who is authorized to represent other people, typically an elected representative at a conference.

desert To abandon a military unit.

empresario Someone who is authorized and given land to start a colony. The empresario recruits settlers for the colony and oversees the colony.

garrison A military fort or base.

joint resolution A resolution in American government that requires a majority vote in both the House and the Senate rather than a two-thirds vote in the Senate.

manifest destiny A philosophy that espouses that it is America's right—indeed, its duty—to expand its territory and spread its way of life.

militia A group of people who are trained like soldiers and organized for military service.

mission A building or group of buildings used to support Christian missionaries.

missionary A person who goes to another country to do religious work, such as convert Native people to the religion.

monarchy A country that is governed by a monarch, such as a king or queen.

mutiny The act of refusing to obey orders and/or to attempt to wrest control away from the person in charge.

pioneer The name given to someone who is among the first to move to a new area.

presidio The name given to forts under Spanish control.

provisional government An interim or temporary government.

republic A country that is governed by elected representatives rather than a monarch.

secede The act of separating from a nation to become a new independent nation.

siege An attack that lasts for a long period of time.

sovereignty Refers to a country's right to govern itself.

Tejano The name given to settlers in Texas of Spanish or Mexican origin.

treaty An agreement made between two or more countries or groups of people.

viceroy An official who is placed in charge of a country, colony, or province as a representative of his or her monarch.

Further Information

Books

Brands, H.W. *Lone Star Nation: The Epic Story of the Battle for Texas Independence.* New York: Anchor Books, 2004.

Greenberg, Amy S. *A Wicked War: Polk, Clay, Lincoln, and the Invasion of Mexico.* New York: Vintage Books, 2012.

Merry, Robert W. *A Country of Vast Designs: James K. Polk, the Mexican War and the Conquest of the American Continent.* New York: Simon and Schuster, 2009.

Websites

A Guide to the Mexican War by the US Library of Congress
www.loc.gov/rr/program/bib/mexicanwar

This site offers access to digital collections at the Library of Congress that pertain to the Mexican-American War, including manuscripts, maps, government documents, and more.

The US-Mexican War
www.dmwv.org/mexwar/mexwar1.htm

Links to images, documents, historic sites, and maps make this site, run by the Descendants of Mexican War Veterans, a destination for anyone who wants to learn more about the Mexican-American War.

The US-Mexican War

www.pbs.org/kera/usmexicanwar/index_flash.html

Visit PBS's site to read about the prelude to the Mexican-American War, the war itself, and the aftermath. You'll also find biographies of key players and a handy timeline.

Museums

The Alamo

Visit the Alamo in San Antonio, site of the famous battle during the Mexican-American War and so-called "Shrine of Texas Dignity."

Bullock Museum

Visit this Austin museum to gain an overview of the history of Texas, including a scale replica of La Salle's *Belle*.

San Jacinto Museum and History

This museum, just twenty minutes from downtown Houston, features interactive exhibits about the eighteen-minute Battle of San Jacinto, the final battle in the Texas Revolution.

Bibliography

"Austin's Colony." Texas A&M University. Accessed July 3, 2015. www.tamu.edu/faculty/ccbn/dewitt/adp/history/ hispanic_period/tenoxtitlan/austins_colony.html.

Barker, Eugene C. "Stephen Fuller Austin." Texas A&M University. Accessed July 6, 2015. www.tamu.edu/faculty/ ccbn/dewitt/adp/history/bios/austin/austin.html.

"The Battle of Huamantla in Huamantla, Tlaxcala." The Mexican American War. Accessed July 6, 2015. mexican-american.american-battlefields.com/ battle/?id=31&n=Battle+of+Huamantla.

"Colonization Through Annexation." Focus on Texas History. Accessed July 3, 2015. www.cah.utexas.edu/ texashistory/annex/index.php?s=2.

"Davy Crockett." Bio.com. Accessed July 3, 2015. www. biography.com/people/davy-crockett-9261693.

Hickman, Kennedy. "Mexican-American War: Major General Zachary Taylor." About.com. Accessed July 6, 2015. militaryhistory.about.com/od/1800sarmybiographies/p/ Mexican-American-War-Major-General-Zachary-Taylor-A-Military-Profile.htm.

History.com. Accessed July 6, 2015. www.history.com.

Horsman, Reginald. *Race and Manifest Destiny: Origins of American Racial Anglo-Saxonism.* Cambridge, MA: Harvard University Press, 1986.

The Inflation Calculator. Accessed July 6, 2015. www.westegg.com/inflation/.

"Manifest Destiny." AP Study Notes.org. Accessed July 3, 2015. www.apstudynotes.org/us-history/topics/manifest-destiny/.

Merriam-Webster Dictionary. Accessed July 6, 2015. www.merriam-webster.com.

Minster, Christopher. "Biography of Stephen F. Austin." About.com. Accessed July 5, 2015. latinamericanhistory.about.com/od/TexasIndependence/p/Biography-Of-Stephen-F-Austin.htm.

"Rene Robert Cavalier: LaSalle's Final Journey." The Mariners' Museum. Accessed July 3, 2015. ageofex.marinersmuseum.org/index.php?type=explorersection&id=131.

The Presidents. Accessed July 3, 2015. www.whitehouse.gov/1600/presidents.

"Sam Houston." Famous Texans. Accessed July 3, 2015. www.famoustexans.com/samhouston.htm.

"The San Jacinto Battle." Something About Everything Military. Accessed July 3, 2015. www.jcs-group.com/military/war1835/sanjacinto.html.

"Teaching with Documents: The Treaty of Guadalupe Hidalgo." National Archives. Accessed July 6, 2015. www. archives.gov/education/lessons/guadalupe-hidalgo/.

Texas Beyond History. Accessed July 3, 2015. www. texasbeyondhistory.net/.

Texas History Timeline. Bullock Museum. Accessed July 3, 2015. www.thestoryoftexas.com/discover/texas-history-timeline.

Texas History Timeline: Key Events in Early Texas. Lone Star Junction. Accessed July 3, 2015. www.lsjunction. com/events/events.htm.

"Texas Lone Star." The University of Texas at Austin. Accessed July 6, 2015. www.utexas.edu/gtc/assets/pdfs/ lonestar.pdf.

Texas State Historical Association. Accessed July 3, 2015. tshaonline.org/.

The Texas State Library and Archives Commission. Accessed July 3, 2015. www.tsl.texas.gov.

US-Mexican War. PBS. Accessed July 3, 2015. www.pbs.org/ kera/usmexicanwar/index_flash.html.

"Victory at San Jacinto: A Dark Time for the Rebellion." The San Jacinto Museum of History. Accessed July 3, 2015. www.sanjacinto-museum.org/The_Battle/Birth_of_a_ Republic/.

Index

Page numbers in **boldface** are illustrations. Entries in **boldface** are glossary terms.

About the Author

Kate Shoup has written more than thirty books and has edited hundreds more. When not working, Kate loves to watch IndyCar racing, ski, read, and ride her motorcycle. She lives in Indianapolis with her husband, her daughter, and their dog. To learn more about Kate and her work, visit www.kateshoup.com.